A E S C H Y L U S
THE ORESTEIA

An Adaptation
by Rob Hardy

To Ruth Weiner

Copyright © 2017 by Rob Hardy.
Published 2017.

Published by Hero Now Theatre, Inc. Minneapolis 55418.

All rights reserved. Except for brief passages quoted in newspaper, magazine, radio, or television reviews, no part of this book may be reproduced in any form or by any means, electronic or mechanical, including photocopying or recording, or by any information storage and retrieval system, without permission in writing from the publisher.

Professionals and amateurs are hereby warned that this material, being fully protected under the Copyright Laws of the United States of America and all other countries of the Berne and Universal Copyright Conventions, is subject to a royalty. All rights for performances, including but not limited to, professional, amateur, recording, motion picture, recitation, lecturing, public reading, radio and television broadcasting, and the rights of translations into foreign languages, are expressly reserved. All inquiries concerning rights, including permission to reprint and performing rights (professional, amateur, and stock), should be addressed to Hero Now Theatre by sending an email to rights@heronowtheatre.org or by visiting the Rights page at www.heronowtheatre.org.

"Introduction: The Fiery Arc of Justice" copyright © 2017 by Thomas Van Nortwick. All rights reserved. Used by permission.

ISBN-13: 978-0-9987882-1-0

Library of Congress Catalog Card Number: 2017935916

Printed in the United States of America.

Contents

Foreword	ix
Introduction: The Fiery Arc of Justice by Thomas Van Nortwick	xv
Publisher's Note	xxv
The Oresteia	1
Notes	69

THE ORESTEIA

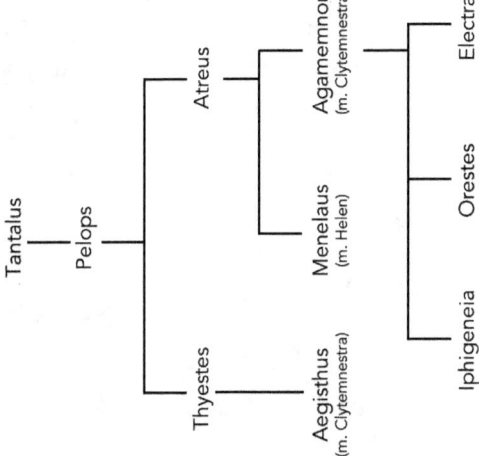

Figure 1. Family tree of Orestes.

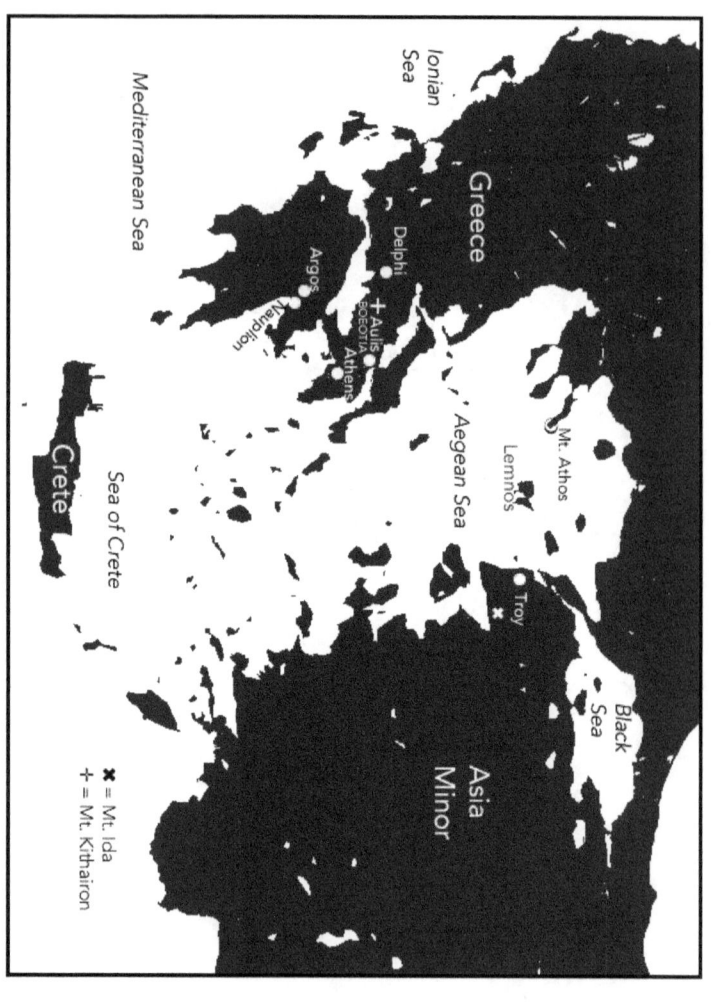

Figure 2. Places in this adaptation of *The Oresteia*.

Foreword

Aeschylus's *Oresteia*, first performed in 458 BCE, comprises three full-length plays: *Agamemnon*, *Choephoroi* (*Libation Bearers*), and *Eumenides*. Ruth Weiner (Class of 1944 Professor of Theater and Liberal Arts, Emerita) commissioned this adaptation for a production at Carleton College in May 2012. Ruth wanted an adaptation that condensed the original trilogy into a single play with a running time of two hours. The goal was a script that would be both manageable for a college production and accessible to a modern audience. The original production involved hundreds of Carleton students as actors and crew members, ran for two weekends, and played to full houses in Carleton's new Weitz Center for Creativity Theater.

This adaptation seeks to preserve the basic outline of Aeschylus's trilogy: the same structure of scenes and choruses, the same story arc that moves from murder and revenge to institutionalized justice in the law courts of Athens. It also preserves much of Aeschylus's imagery and symbolism: fire and blood, the lion and the snake, the oppositions of male and female that play out in the confrontation between Apollo and the Furies. At the same time, I attempted to create my own poetic idiom for retelling the story of the Oresteia. As Eric Dugdale noted in his review of the original production in the journal *Didaskalia*, this adaptation "offers a stripped-down style in which every word counts and immediacy trumps Aeschylean grandeur."

When Ruth Weiner and I visited Athens in March 2011, we attended a modern Greek production of Harold Pinter's *The Caretaker*. Pinter is about as far as you can get from Greek tragedy: his plots are relatively simple and commonplace, his language is mundane and colloquial. Greek tragedy on the other hand is elevated and stylized, far removed from the everyday into the realm of the mythical. I wanted to convey that sense of the mythical and stylized, while still using language that would be accessible to audiences more accustomed to contemporary drama. The result should be both strange, as the ancient Greeks are often strange to us, and familiar, as many of the issues that concerned the Greeks are familiar to us.

In this adaptation, I have attempted to preserve three distinct but overlapping narrative modes at work in Greek tragedy. The plot of the *Oresteia*—the return of Agamemnon from Troy and the subsequent fate of the house of Atreus—has its origins in ancient epic, in the stories that bards like Homer told of the heroes of Greek prehistory. The poetic storytelling of Homeric epic, translated into the words and actions of characters on the stage, is one of the narrative modes at work in the tragedy. At the same time, the choruses arise out of the hymns and liturgical dances of Greek religion. Greek tragedy was performed in the context of a religious festival, the annual festival of Dionysus, and retains a strong flavor of the solemnity and celebration of ritual. The choruses are also storytellers, telling the shared stories and performing the shared rituals that bind the Athenians together as a community. Finally, the interaction between the characters onstage—the accusation, interrogation, dialogue, and debate—has an affinity with the argumentative mode of the law courts, the assembly, and the philosophical schools of ancient Athens. All three of these modes—the epic, hymnic, and argumentative—are highly formal and public, and correspond to the three public spaces in which the action of the play takes place: in front of the doors of Agamemnon's palace in Argos, in the sanctuary of Apollo at Delphi, and in the law court of the Areopagus in Athens.

Those familiar with Aeschylus's original will find some things missing from this adaptation—some peculiarly Aeschylean turns of phrase, for example—and will notice changes made in the treatment of the chorus. In the original trilogy, each of the three plays had a different chorus: the old men of Argos in the Agamemnon, mourning women in the *Choephoroi*, the Furies in *Eumenides*. Because this adaptation condenses the trilogy into a single play, I chose to have the citizens of Argos of

Agammemnon and *Choephoroi* transform into the Furies of *Eumenides*. For me, this underscores an important theme in the play: the role communities have in perpetuating violence, in pursuing justice, and in choosing to submit to the rule of law. The play begins as a story of domestic violence focusing on the fates of the individual members of Agamemnon's family, but becomes a story about the effects of violence and the possibilities of reconciliation in the community as a whole.

The original Carleton production of this adaptation was part of the Kennedy Center American College Theater Festival, and was reviewed in *Didaskalia*, a journal dedicated to Greek and Roman drama in performance. In conjunction with the production, I participated in a workshop on Greek tragedy at Arcadia Charter School in Northfield, Minnesota, and taught a course on the *Oresteia* for the Cannon Valley Elder Collegium. These outreach efforts were nominated for an Outreach Award from the Society for Classical Studies. The production was also the focus of a interdisciplinary course at Carleton in the spring of 2012, "The Oresteia Project: Visualizing Greek Tragedy," taught by Ruth Weiner (Theater and Dance) and Clara Shaw Hardy (Classics). This was my second collaboration with Ruth Weiner on the production of a Greek tragedy; the first was a production of my translation of Eurpides' *Iphigeneia at Aulis* at Carleton College in May 2000.

The adaptation received its second performance in September 2016, in a production by Hero Now Theatre in Zoran Mojsilov's outdoor sculpture garden in northeast Minneapolis. This production included nightly talk-backs with the cast, pre-show talks for students from local colleges, and a CLE (continuing legal education) panel discussion arranged through the Mitchell Hamline School of Law.

I would like to thank everyone who has been involved in the development, production, and publication of this script. Special thanks to Ruth Weiner and Clara Shaw Hardy (Carleton College), Thomas Van Nortwick (Oberlin College), and David Severtson, Kristin Halsey, and Peter Aitchison (Hero Now Theatre).

Rob Hardy
Northfield, Minnesota
November 2016

This adaptation of Aeschylus's Oresteia was first performed at the Weitz Center for Creativity Theater, Carleton College, May 11–13 and 18–20, 2012, with the following cast:

Watchman	Patrick Stephen
Speaking Chorus	Rachel Porcher, Shavera Seneviratne, Ben Stroup
Non-Speaking Chorus/Dancers	Emily Ban, Rebecca Brown, Kristen Dooley, Torre Edhal, Elise Erickson, Rebecca Feldman, Amelia Harris, Sara Klugman, Hannah Lucal, Marisa Luck, Gustave Maisonrouge, Roman Morris, Deborah Tan, Hannah Joy Wirshing, Molly Work, Winnie Zwick
Clytemnestra	Chelsea Lau
Messenger	Soren Hopkins
Agamemnon	Dan Peck
Cassandra	Jessica Morrison
Aegisthus	Nikhil Pandey
Guards/Attendants	Will Grey, Miles Douglas
Young Electra	Isabel Aylin
Orestes	Josh Davids
Electra	Emily Altschul
Pythia	Harper Makowsky
Apollo	Chris Densmore
Athena	Rachel Linder

Director: Ruth Weiner
Music: Mary Ellen Childs
Choreography: Judith Howard & Semaphore Dance Company
Lighting Design: Jeffrey Bartlett & Tony Stoeri
Video Design: Paul Bernhardt
Makeup and Costume Design: Mary Ellen Kelling
Scenic Design: Joe Stanley

The first professional production of this adaptation was staged by Hero Now Theatre in Minneapolis, Minnesota, September 9–12, 2016, and September 15, 16, and 18, 2016, in the outdoor sculpture garden of Zoran Mojsilov in northeast Minneapolis with the following cast:

Watchman	Corey DiNardo
Chorus A	McKinnley Aitchison
Chorus B	Ashley Hovell
Chorus C	Lindy Jackson
Non-Speaking Chorus/Dancers	Emily Gustafson, Hannah Kuduk
Clytemnestra	Katherine Kupiecki
Messenger	Michael Turner
Agamemnon	Peter Aitchison
Cassandra	Madeline Achen
Aegisthus	Matt Englund
Orestes	Vincent Hannam
Electra	Annie Colling
Pythia	Kristin Halsey
Apollo	Kip Dooley
Athena	Danielle Kiminski

Director: Kristin Halsey
Drums: Jake Stien
Set, costume, and lighting design: Kristin Halsey

All actors other than those taking the named Chorus parts took on additional roles as Chorus members, guards, and attendants when not playing their named roles.

Introduction
The Fiery Arc of Justice

Just before leaving the stage, the chorus members of Rob Hardy's masterful adaptation of Aeschylus's *Oresteia* change from their Fury costumes to modern street clothes. (Hardy imagines them donning "Black Lives Matter" or "Pride" T-shirts.) The enormous arc of Aeschlylus's original dramatic vision, which begins with the news of Troy's fall relayed across the Aegean via signal-fires and ends with torch-bearers filing out of the Theater of Dionysus in fifth-century BCE Athens, now stretches yet further in Hardy's reimagining, finally coming to rest right here, right now. With this gesture, Hardy signals that like the Athenians, we must learn from a troubled past if we are to move forward in a fruitful way. Aeschylus's bold vision traces the origins of fledgling democracy of his own time back through centuries to the mythic expedition of Agamemnon and his Greek army to retrieve Helen from Paris, her Trojan abductor. The complex forces that shape that journey and its bloody aftermath—divine will, fate, the murky intentions of flawed mortals—are often mysterious. But the evolution they signify, from a society bound together by blood ties, dominated by a few wealthy clans, to the world's first democracy, comes through clearly in Aeschylus's trilogy. Fresh from their second triumph over the Persians in thirty years, the citizens of fifth-century Athens took pride in the redistribution of power and status that their democratic reforms had effected. This restructuring was accompanied in turn by a fundamental reexamination by Athenian artists and intellectuals of how a human life was to be evaluated. One of its first and proudest artistic documents is Aeschylus's *Oresteia*.

In 458, when *Oresteia* was first produced, Athenian democracy was barely fifty years old. Cleisthenes, the last of the Athenian "tyrants"—that is, men who established themselves with support from the poorer citizens in the face of the traditional coalitions of wealthy aristocrats—instituted a set of reforms in 508–7 that undercut the power of blood ties in the exercise of political power in Athens. He divided the four traditional tribes (Geleontes, Hopletes, Argadeis, and Aegicoreis), bound together by family alliances, into ten new groups, defined geographically. He also established local "demes" (from the Greek *demos*, meaning either a country district, as opposed to the city, or "common people") composed of several small hamlets, a village, or a suburb, each with its own assembly and leader. Each of the ten new tribes was to have two demes from each of the three traditional geographic areas of Athens and the surrounding countryside: the city of Athens, the inland farms, and the coastal villages. The effect of these reforms was to weaken the old family alliances, articulated through blood ties, in favor of a new distribution of political power based on location. Athenian democracy (*demos* + *kratos*, "rule by the people") was born out of these changes.

The victories over the Persians, of which the Athenians were so proud, also helped to spur the development of the new democracy. The Athenian navy, which at the height of its power had 400 ships and as many as 80,000 men, was instrumental in the defeat of the second Persian invasion. The rowers who powered those ships were mostly recruited from the poorer classes, and the contribution of this part of the populace to the city's safety brought pressure after 480 to extend the democratic reforms. Finally, in 461, Ephialtes, an Athenian general and leader of the radical democratic faction, put into place a set of reforms that brought Athenian democracy to its mature form. He was able to carry measures stripping the aristocratic court, which met on the Areopagus ("hill of Ares"), of its political power and to establish the dominance of the Ecclesia (the Popular Assembly), the Boule (Council), and new law courts. All of these changes widened the distribution of political power and undercut the influence of wealthy aristocratic families.

From the same restless genius that created the world's first democracy also came the first drama in recorded history. The exact origins of Athenian tragedy are unclear, but however the genre evolved, its constituent parts—mythical stories of heroes often paralleled in epic poetry and choral songs in the dialect of choral lyric—suggest some kind of amalgam of those forms. Perhaps what we know as drama came into being when someone combined a speaker with a chorus and had both sides disguised as characters from old myths. Tradition has Thespis, a sixth-century poet, as the first to represent a character in a play and also the first playwright to present a tragedy at the Dionysiac festival in Athens, in 534. Characteristically for the intensely competitive Athenians, the venue for tragic plays (and some comic ones) was the public religious festival in honor of the god Dionysus, where three playwrights were chosen to present their work as part of an annual contest.

The name of Phrynichus, a pupil of Thespis, has also come down to us as an early composer of tragic drama. Not one of his plays survives, but we have nine titles, including *The Sack of Miletus* (492), about the destruction by the Persians of a city on the coast of Asia Minor in the decade before the first invasion of Athens, and *The Phoenissae* (476), celebrating the defeat of the Persians at Salamis four years earlier. Aeschylus was born around 525 in the deme of Eleusis, about fifteen miles from Athens. He fought in both of the wars against the Persians, composed between seventy and ninety plays, and died sometime around 456. His first surviving work, *The Persians*, which seems to have been modeled after *The Phoenissae of Phrynichus*, won first prize at the Dionysiac festival in 472. Six other plays survive, all of which apparently won first prize: *The Seven Against Thebes* (467), *Suppliants* (463), the *Oresteia* trilogy (*Agamemnon*, *Libation Bearers*, *Eumenides*, 458), and *Prometheus Bound* (457?). The authorship of the last play has been much disputed, but the majority of scholars attribute it to Aeschylus.

When the *Oresteia* first appeared in the Theater of Dionysus, on the south side of the Acropolis, Athenian confidence was at its peak. The two victories over the Persian invaders seemed to them to signal the superiority of their democratic city-state over the dissolute monarchs and their minions. Under their leadership, the cities on the mainland and various islands off the coast of Asia Minor in 478 formed a defensive alliance to guard against another invasion. The members could contribute either ships or money to the common treasury, which was initially housed on the island of Delos. As time went on, the contributions were increasingly monetary and were transferred from Delos to Athens in 454. These funds became the main resource for Pericles's spectacular building program on the Acropolis in the 440s, which produced many beautiful monuments, including the Parthenon, with its giant statue of Athena, patron deity of the city. The famous carved friezes along the pediment of that temple depict scenes from the mythical past, celebrating Athenian greatness.

This glorious efflorescence, alas, was soon imperiled by disputes between Athens and her neighboring city-states on the mainland of Greece, leading to the outbreak in 431 of the Peloponnesian War between Athens and Sparta. The conflict lasted twenty-seven years, ending with the defeat and surrender of Athens in 404. The terrible strains on the people of Athens and the surrounding countryside brought by repeated Spartan invasions, plus a plague that ravaged Athens from 430 to 426, are reflected in many powerful tragic dramas by Aeschylus's successors, Sophocles and Euripides, and by Thucydides, whose history of the Peloponnesian War remains our most important source for the history of Athens in the late fifth century. The great period of Athenian tragedy came to an end, perhaps not coincidentally, soon after the defeat by Sparta. Sophocles and Euripides both died in 406, fifty years after the death of Aeschylus. Athens continued to present revivals of old tragedies in the fourth century, but there is no record of new plays being produced at the Dionysiac festival.

It is perhaps not surprising that Athenian tragedy died out after Athens fell from its position of political prominence, since there has probably never been an art form so central to the political, social, and religious practices of any city. The plays were performed at a yearly religious festival in late March, sacred to the god Dionysus, whose altar stood in the center of the performance space of the theater. Wealthy citizens trained and paid the chorus as a civic duty. The performances were open to all male citizens, and probably to women as well. In this expansive, open-air spectacle, Athenians saw the central issues of the day refracted through a mythical lens. A few plays, such as Aeschylus's *The Persians* or Phrynichus's *The Phoenissae*, took historical events as their subject, but much more common was the practice of drawing from heroic legends set in the distant past, the cycle of stories surrounding the Trojan War and its aftermath, the Theban sagas of Oedipus and his family, or the adventures of Herakles. Likewise, relatively few plays were actually set in Athens, but the issues dramatized on stage always directly or indirectly reflected contemporary life in the city, the fear and suffering from the plague in Sophocles's *Oedipus Rex*, the challenges raised by new laws about citizenship in his *Women of Trachis*, the misery of women left at the mercy of conquerors in Euripides's *Trojan Women*.

The form itself of the plays, illustrious heroes interacting with a chorus of more ordinary people, encouraged probing of one central issue for the Athenians: how to accommodate conspicuous individuals within the new communal focus of their democratic system. The hero returning from war to find his household and family estranged by his absence is one of the most common figures in Greek myth and legend. Soldiers in fifth-century Athens might well face the same challenges, but in any event the advent of democracy presented the same dilemma every day. Evolving from a political system bound together by alliances between wealthy families to one open to and influenced by all free citizens in a mere fifty years was bound to stir things up, for good or ill. Beyond issues of political power, there is a yet more fundamental question: if blood ties do not confer worth in and of themselves, how then to evaluate a human life? The vibrant intellectual ferment of the fifth century in Athens, with its lasting impact on western civilization, focused on many fundamental issues, but none more important than this. Athenian tragedy and comedy, the histories of Herodotus and Thucydides, the speculation of Pre-Socratic philosophers, all finally address in one way or another the question of what it means to be human. Sophists, traveling teachers who came through Athens in the mid- to late fifth century, claimed to be able to teach anyone willing to listen to achieve the excellence that had earlier been thought to be conferred only by birth. Socrates roamed the Agora provoking citizens to argue with him over justice, the nature of truth, the relationship of knowledge to virtue. So influential was he that the citizens of Athens eventually put him on trial and sentenced him to death for corrupting the youth of the city.

In the midst of all this, on a March morning in 458, the *Oresteia* had its first performance. The audience would have filed into the seats carved into the south slope of the Acropolis, looking down at the circular (or rectangular, the evidence is unclear) *orchestra*, or "dancing place," eighty-seven feet across. At the back edge was a temporary wooden stage building, the *skēnē*, which this day would have been the royal palace in Argos, then later the shrine of Apollo in Delphi, and finally a building on the hill of the Areopagus in Athens. There was a wide doorway in the middle of the building, through which actors, but not the chorus, could enter and exit (there must also have been a hidden back entrance to the building). No scenes in Athenian tragedy are set indoors, though some of the audience would have been able to see a little way into the interior of the skēnē, if the doors were open, as if peeking indoors. Through these doors we would have glimpsed the slaughtered corpses of Agamemnon and his concubine Cassandra at the end of *Agamemnon*, then of Clytemnestra and her lover Aegisthus at the end of *Libation Bearers*. In the middle of the orchestra stood some kind of raised stone, probably an altar to Dionysus but available to signify various other things in the play being performed. Along both sides of this building were entrance paths, *eisodoi*, where actors and chorus would enter and exit. There would probably have been no raised stage between the skēnē and the orchestra in the fifth century. The crowd would have been large, perhaps as many as 6000—Aeschylus at the height of his powers would have been a big draw.

Lying on top of the skēnē, a lonely sentinel, scanning the sky. He was masked, as were all the players in Athenian drama. After his first speech, the chorus would enter, twelve figures moving in unison to a marching rhythm. Their robes could have been brilliantly colored, catching the morning sun as they made their way in, though on this morning they were elders of Argos, who might have been more subdued. In general, we must imagine that there was bright color everywhere in Athens, buildings and sculptures painted red, blue, yellow. Our idea of what ancient Mediterranean cities looked like comes from marble that has lost its bright paint, so we imagine the Greeks strolling around against a blinding white backdrop, striking poses, but anyone who has been in Greece knows that sky was made for brilliant color. Once the chorus had entered and formed up in the middle of the orchestra, the play would proceed with choral songs, chanting and dancing accompanied by a flute and/or lyre, alternating with spoken dialogue between the actors and the chorus. In almost all extant Athenian tragedy, the chorus would remain in the orchestra for the entire drama, marching off at the very end. This afternoon, in fact, would have been an exception, because the chorus of the third play in the trilogy, *Eumenides*, leaves the stage and returns with a change in scene—another rarity in Athenian tragedy. The whole trilogy would have taken somewhere around six hours to produce, assuming breaks between plays. There was no artificial lighting for performances, and we would have seen the entire spectacle before sunset, which would have been about 6:30. But perhaps Aeschylus would have wanted to have the Furies, now called the Eumenides, "the kindly ones," make their final exit carrying torches, so planning to end at dusk might have provided a more powerful tableau.

Since no stage directions have come down to us with the original Greek texts, nor any information about the music or dance movements of the chorus, our ideas about how plays might have been staged must rely on other kinds of evidence, from the texts themselves, including notes made later in the margins of manuscripts ("scholia"), from archaeological finds on the site of the Theater of Dionysus, and from representations in Greek art. But finally, much imagination is required. And appropriately enough, because the conventions that governed the form of the plays—no interiors, all major physical action represented as happening off stage and reported via messenger speeches, masked players so that individualized facial expressions were not possible—demanded that the original audience exercise considerable imagination. In doing so, they would have participated in the creation of a play's meaning for themselves much more than can we who sit before computer-generated explosions. Aristotle, writing a century after the great tragedies were produced, claimed that the experience of watching tragedy promoted an intense emotional involvement of the audience in the events on stage, which in turn produced "catharsis," a vicarious and salubrious cleansing of emotions. A "Life of Aeschylus," written two centuries after his death, also claimed in an apocryphal but telling tidbit that women in the audience of the first performance of *Eumenides* suffered miscarriages.

However we may envision the spectacle in the Theater of Dionysus, it's clear that recreating anything like the original conditions of performance would be impossible today. Translations of the original Greek text are still used to stage the trilogy, but certain aspects of such performances will always be problematic. First, there is the chorus, always a challenge for modern productions. We do not have any useful analogue in our culture for the communal voice of the chorus in Athenian tragedy. The closest approximations might be the choruses in nineteenth-century opera or Broadway musicals, but the impact of those media is vastly different from tragic choruses. Masked actors are another problem for us, since we are so used to evaluating character through facial expressions.

(And masks also now conjure associations that would be distracting, African ritual, costume balls—opera again, and so forth.) More specific to the *Oresteia* are the daunting length of the trilogy—modern productions of Sophocles's *Electra*, which covers approximately the same part of the story as *Libation Bearers*, are more frequent than those of the trilogy—and Aeschylus's dense symbolic and allusive language, especially in the choruses. The entrance song and first chorus of *Agamemnon* are over 220 lines in the original Greek text, the second chorus around 150 lines. The challenges, for modern actors of chanting in unison on that scale (never mind dancing), and for the audience to follow the exposition of the mythical background for the story, are daunting.

Despite all of these formidable challenges, of scale, form, and language, Aeschylus's drama is still performed today. The power of his ideas and their relevance to our own world are such that actors and directors find their own way to bring the plays to the stage. Rob Hardy's reimagining of the trilogy is particularly bold in its response to the demands of modern production. He has produced a single play, lasting around two hours, which retains all the major themes of the trilogy. The characteristic structure of all of Aeschylus's plays—the chorus first supplying the mythical background for the action, then a central symbolic scene that sets the terms of the drama's argument (e.g., the tapestry scene in *Agamemnon*), followed by the working out of the implications of the central symbols—is preserved in micro in his treatment of each of the original plays. His chorus is a flexible instrument, three or more actors who divide the lines of choral response with the possibility of adding non-speaking dancers, thus avoiding the chanting in unison that so often makes the choruses of modern versions of Athenian tragedy sound portentously bombastic. His language is supple and clear, while retaining much of the original imagery that spans the trilogy. (See his foreword for further details.)

Hardy's mastery of Aeschylus's poetic and dramatic vision is evident in the final trial scene, where the Furies play the role of prosecutors of Orestes, Apollo speaks for the defense, and Athena becomes the judge. This section of *Eumenides*, final play of the trilogy, is often puzzling to a modern audience. We are trained on reruns of *Law and Order* and so expect substantive arguments, clever traps set for unsuspecting witnesses, objections shouted out from the opposing side. Aeschylus's scene is more like two groups of students in a schoolyard, taunting each other, trading insults without much attention to rhetorical exposition. Not that this exchange fails to present the essence of the multilayered dispute that has dominated all three plays. On the contrary, the intricately linked chains of imagery that span the entire trilogy are brought to bear in Aeschylus's characteristically bold symbolic language, so that the crucial evolution in Athenian social and political order in the fifth century, refracted through myth and sanctioned by the gods, comes brilliantly before us. But this idiom is so alien to most of us that the true power of the resolution can be lost in its original form. Hardy's exchanges present the essence of the conflict in his own poetic medium, but in a form much more accessible to modern audiences.

The heart of Aeschylus's huge dramatic edifice, what has carried its power to move audiences through the millennia down to the present, is the movement from a seemingly endless cycle of revenge, between families and across generations, whose allegiances are cemented by blood ties, to a new system in which a third party, which stands outside of the two warring sides, can resolve the conflict by compromise. On the mythic level, the strife is between different elements of the family of Atreus, father of Agamemnon and uncle of Aegisthus, Clytemnestra's lover. The third party is a newly constituted court, made up of Athenian citizens, who hold the first trial. For Athenians of the fifth century, the family represented on one level the aristocratic clans who had dominated their political and social order for centuries, while the third party was the new democratic city-state, the workings of which were dramatized by the resolution emerging from the trial scene. It is no accident that the first trial was imagined to take place on the hill of the Areopagus. In a kind of mythic and historical syllogism, Ephialtes's emasculation of the old aristocratic court in 461 is to the new democratic order as the establishment of that same court in the misty past was to the end of private, inter-familial justice. In that sense, the real hero in Aeschylus's trilogy is Athenian democracy.

As we have noted, Rob Hardy envisions his chorus of Furies shedding their frightening costumes to appear at play's end in contemporary dress, with "Black Lives Matter" or "Pride" on their T-shirts. Thus, in his vision, the vast arc of Aeschylus's drama stretches from the mythic past not just to the fifth century, but to this very day. Our own beleaguered democracy is undergoing serious challenges at the beginning of the twenty-first century. Channeling Aeschylus, Rob Hardy encourages us to imagine what new form of justice can free us from our own self-created political and social dilemmas.

Thomas Van Nortwick
Oberlin, Ohio
December 2016

Publisher's Note

On the evening of April 4, 1968, Robert F. Kennedy interrupted his candidacy for president of the United States to announce to supporters in Indianapolis that Martin Luther King Jr. had been shot and killed. Delivering a speech from the podium on a flatbed truck, Kennedy favored his own heart-felt words over those prepared by his campaign staff and ignored police warnings about the possibility of riots, which by then were spreading elsewhere throughout the nation. About halfway through his impassioned plea for "compassion toward one another," he recited these words from Aeschylus's *Agamemnon*:

> Even in our sleep, pain which cannot forget
> falls drop by drop upon the heart,
> until, in our own despair,
> against our will,
> comes wisdom
> through the awful grace of God.

Asking his followers to "say a prayer for our country," Kennedy encouraged the nation to "dedicate ourselves to what the Greeks wrote so many years ago: to tame the savageness of man and make gentle the life of this world."

In that same year the Guthrie Theater in Minneapolis staged John Lewin's three-act adaptation of Aeschylus's trilogy *The Oresteia*, whose first play is *Agamemnon*. Lewin had worked on *The House of Atreus* earlier in the 1960s, and published it with the University of Minnesota

Press in 1966, but the American war in Vietnam would have provided a fitting backdrop to the Guthrie's production. In the story of Argos and the effects of its long conflict with Troy one could undoubtedly discern an ancient admonishment that would afflict the hearts of theatergoers.

Many adaptations of Aeschylus's trilogy exist, but in publishing Rob Hardy's poetic, skillful version, Hero Now Theatre nominates it as a worthy successor to Lewin's, which is now in its fifties, and a worthy competitor to other, more recent productions. Hero Now gave Rob's script its first professional production in September 2016 in Minneapolis, finding that it spoke forcefully to our own roiled times. Kristin Halsey staged the play outdoors among sculptures and granite columns that evoked the ruins of Athens, and audiences, whom we asked to vote as the jury in the play, stayed after to discuss such topics as whether legal process confers social healing, whether a legal system can accommodate all the values a society professes, and how Greek ideas of justice differ from or resemble our own.

Because of its quality and its abundant relevance to our age, Rob's script deserves to reach a large readership and more audiences. Like Lewin's, Rob's adaptation strives to be a compelling theatrical experience, and it succeeds in being a play that other companies will want to produce. It succeeds in its literary appeal. As a published poet and critic, Rob brings a sensitivity to language and a sharp eye for dramatic structure. Like Lewin Rob is less interested in fidelity to Greek theatrical customs (with which modern audiences are unfamiliar). As Tyrone Guthrie wrote in his short essay in *The House of Atreus*, scholastic fidelity to Aeschylus is "not necessarily the supreme virtue for a stage version." But as a classicist Rob keeps a steady eye on the tradition that Aeschylus forged.

Also, unlike Lewin's adaptation, which stresses the trilogy's mythic component and gives a great deal of space to the chorus, Rob's version is more visceral. This is the story of the individuals who killed and were killed, the jealousies, erratic behaviors, and flawed decisions of a royal bloodline of a distant time, while including the mythic elements required to understand the story. The chorus remains—to offer comment, to advance the story—but is given less prominence. And, in the story of Orestes's actions and his trial before the Athenian jury, we see an enactment of the journey that Greek society underwent, from a society where justice was meted out through familial revenge killings to one based on a system of courts and law.

This last thing may be the element that modern audiences will struggle to comprehend. The question of Orestes's guilt or innocence is argued on grounds very different from those on which our courts function. Yet, in discussing this topic with audiences after they had submitted their own votes, we believe they grasped something about how different societies face their political and legal quandaries their own way—and how precarious their solutions can be.

Hero Now Theatre launches its publishing program with this volume. Thank you to Springboard for the Arts of Saint Paul, Minnesota, for the use of equipment used in the preparation of this, our first book. We encourage other theaters to produce the play (send inquiries to rights@heronowtheatre.org), and we hope Rob's beautiful script can help us in our incessant struggle to bring us wisdom and to tame this savage world.

David L. Severtson
Executive Director
Hero Now Theatre
February 2017

THE ORESTEIA

Characters (*in order of appearance*)
Watchman.
Chorus A, **Chorus B**, **Chorus C** (see note).
Clytemnestra, wife of Agamemnon, lover of Aegisthus, mother of
  Iphigeneia, Orestes, and Electra.
Messenger, a Greek soldier returning from Troy with Agamemnon.
Agamemnon, king of Argos and commander of the Greek forces
  at Troy, absent from his home for ten years of war. Husband of
  Clytemnestra, father of Iphigeneia, Orestes, and Electra.
Cassandra, daughter of Priam, king of Troy, taken as a prize by Agamemnon after the fall of Troy.
Aegisthus, cousin of Agamemnon and lover of Clytemnestra.
Electra, daughter of Agamemnon and Clytemnestra.
Orestes, son of Agamemnon and Clytemnestra. In exile near Delphi at
  the beginning of the play.
Pythia, the priestess and oracle of Apollo at Delphi.
Apollo, Greek god, spokesman for his father Zeus and advocate for
  Orestes.
Athena, Greek goddess, patroness of the city of Athens.

Non-speaking
Young Electra, a child of ten or eleven.
Dancers, or Non-Speaking Chorus Members (see note).
Guards.
Jurors.

Note on the Chorus: In the script, the Chorus lines are divided among three speaking Chorus members. At the discretion of the collaborators, the Chorus lines can be divided differently, and additional speaking members of the Chorus can be added depending on resources. As in Carleton's production, the speaking Chorus may be augmented by a chorus of dancers. If there are no dancers, non-speaking Chorus members can be used where dancers are specified in the script.

Act I

Argos. In keeping with the conventions of ancient Greek theater, the focus is on the doors of the palace. There should be a platform above the doors, where the Watchman—and later Clytemnestra and Athena—will appear. Otherwise, the stage should be kept relatively bare.

Voice-over, whispering the opening lines of Aeschylus's play in Greek.[1] The Watchman appears on the roof of the palace.

Watchman.[2] Who's there?

(*He lights a match, but the wind blows it out. The whispering stops.*)

It must have been the wind.

Sometimes I swear I can hear voices.
The night plays tricks on my brain.
I reach out my hands and touch nothing but darkness.
I start to imagine that none of this is real.
These stone walls, these damp clothes,
the woman who sends me here to watch,
the war that took the Greeks across the sea—
maybe none of this is real. In the morning
I'll find myself alone in some empty space.
I stand here night after night watching
the same stars turning through the sky.

Every now and then one of them falls
from its place and burns out across the night.
It must mean something. And sometimes
I amuse myself by looking for patterns in the stars.
There. (*Pointing up.*) That group of stars looks like a bear.
Do you see it? (*Tracing the air with his finger.*) No?

It's no wonder I imagine things. It's no wonder
I sometimes hear voices. For ten years
I've stood alone on this roof top, watching
for a beacon kindled from the flames of Troy.

(*Beneath him, two Chorus members, Chorus A and B, enter from the left and right.*)

Chorus A.
Ten years since Agamemnon marched
hell-bent through the Lion Gate,[3] cursing Helen
and calling for the blood of Priam and all his sons.

Watchman.
Ten years collecting dew and shivering with cold.

Chorus B.
Ten years since the Greeks assembled at Aulis,[4]
sharpening their spears and waiting
for a wind to launch their thousand ships.

Watchman.
Ten years of hearing every slammed door,
every cry of pain or pleasure from the house below.

Chorus A.
Ten years since Calchas said the first blood
of the war would be a Greek girl's,
spilled to satisfy the wrath of Artemis,
who kept the wind from the Achaian sails.[5]

Watchman.
Ten years of watching the phases of the moon:
the new moon as modest as a girl,
the waxing moon pregnant with light,
the waning moon sharpened like a blade above the house.

(*The palace doors open, and Chorus C steps out of the doorway. She's wearing a mask and carrying a torch. The doors close behind her.*)

Ten years ago I stood here and watched Iphigeneia[6]
carry the bridal torch through these palace doors.
She was as modest as the new moon.
The only sorrow she knew was in the songs
she sang in the evening, to her father's guests,
when their brains were heavy with wine.
She didn't understand how they looked at her,
or what lust and cruelty was in their hearts.

Agamemnon told her she would be a bride.
She went from the house to meet her husband
with flowers in her hair, like an unplowed meadow,
like a heifer wreathed for sacrifice.
If she trembled, and if her step was hesitant,
it was from fear of the unknown life that awaited her.
She had heard her mother's screams in childbirth,
seen the bloody bed sheets, held the baby Orestes
still slick with his mother's blood.
She thought marriage must be a slow murder.
But she knew that she herself came from her mother's blood.
She knew that, somehow, this was what made life possible.
So she went to meet her husband with a terrified joy.

(*Chorus C sets her torch in a torch holder at the front of the stage.*)

But when she reached the altar, her father bound
her hands and feet, and held a knife to her throat,

and called on Artemis to receive his sacrifice.
And with her last breath, Iphigeneia cried out—

Chorus C. Clytemnestra!

(*Exit Watchman. The doors of the palace open and Clytemnestra enters.*)

Clytemnestra (*raising her hands to the fire*). At last!

(*Addressing the Chorus.*) Troy is fallen!

Chorus A. When did this happen?

Clytemnestra. Tonight.

Chorus B. How do you know this?

Clytemnestra.
My husband set a beacon-keeper to watch on Mount Ida.
The fire he kindled there reproduced the sign of Troy's destruction.
From Mount Ida, the signal passed to Lemnos,
and from Lemnos to Mount Athos,[7] breeding generations
of fire across Greece until this newest flame was kindled here in Argos.
The meaning of these flames is clear: Troy has fallen.

Chorus A. Impossible.

Clytemnestra. It's what happened.

Chorus B. It's something you dreamed.

Clytemnestra. This is no dream.

Chorus A. A delusion.

Chorus B. A false hope.

Chorus C.
You've been living too long in the hope
of Agamemnon's return.

Chorus B.
Hope is like staring too long into the sun.
Its image floats in front of everything.
It becomes a stain on reality.

Clytemnestra.
You treat me like a child!
Would you speak this way to Agamemnon?
It's as clear to me as it would be to any man
who has the eyes to see and a mind to understand:
these flames are a sign that Troy has fallen. (*Chorus turns away.*)
Choose to believe me or not,
events will bear out the truth of what I say.
And when the time comes, it won't find me unprepared.

Gods! I pray that this fire kindled
from the destruction of Troy
will burn kindly here on the hearth of Argos.
I pray that Greeks in their triumph will act
with moderation and self-control,
and let no outrage follow them home to Greece.

(*Clytemnestra enters the palace and the doors close behind her. The dancers enter, carrying urns and placing them around the edges of the stage, or on either side of the palace doors, during the following chorus. Chorus C places her mask among the urns.*)

Chorus A.[8]
Scattered across the plain of Troy,
the fires were like stars burning out—
each fire a body burning,
each one a world coming to an end.
Smoke spread like night across the plain,

blackened the city walls and rose,
like the dark specter of an army
raising its siege engines to the walls:
as smoke the Greeks first entered Troy.
Now each ship that sails from Troy
brings home its cargo of ashes.
The men who left home in bright helmets
and breastplates of shining bronze
come home again in little pots of clay.

Chorus B.
For ten years
the women have waited,
husbanding their fields and farms,
counting their losses,
looking up from their work
to see black sails on the horizon.
A generation has fallen at Troy,
another generation in Greece has grown up fatherless.
Little boys have grown up thinking absence
is what it means to be a man.
Little girls have grown up learning
the name of Helen like a curse.
The birds that descend on the new-sown fields
are Helen's fault; the month without rain,
the hen that stops laying,
the wind that blows dust in the door—
Helen is the name of every misfortune.
The flames that dance
destruction through the streets of Troy
first burned in the mind of Zeus
when Paris came
and carried Helen from her husband's bed.
The anger of Zeus followed him home like a lighted fuse.

Chorus C.
And after Helen went the Greeks:

walled cities emptied of their men,
forests stripped to build the fleet,
cattle butchered, fields laid bare,
treasuries plundered of their bronze—
the wealth of Greece sent as a dowry of war.
Now every home that sent a man to Troy
has its urn, a handful of ashes paid
for what was once a husband, or a son.
Is this how Agamemnon honors
the debt he owes to the women of Greece?

Chorus A.
What will be born of the grievance
Clytemnestra bears against him
for the death of their daughter Iphigeneia?

(*The Messenger enters. He kneels down and kisses the ground. He stands up and walks to the door of the palace and slowly runs his hand over it.*)

Messenger.[9] Can this be real?

Chorus C. You have news from Troy?

Messenger. There is no Troy.

Chorus A. What happened?

Chorus B. Tell us everything.

Messenger. The war is over.

Chorus (*unison*). The war is over!

Messenger.
Those words sound strange to me.
It doesn't seem real.
How can it be over?

For ten years the war was life
and death to the Greeks.
It was everything we knew.
It feels as if I've been through
the end of the world,
and I don't belong to this new world
that's taken its place.

How can I explain what it was like
to someone who wasn't there?
I would need a new language.
Words made of fire and blood,
words that cut and burn.

Sometimes we would see Helen
standing on the ramparts of Troy,
like a flame, like desire itself,
and all we wanted
was to bring our fire to those walls
and force our way inside.
We burned and bled for those walls,
day and night, for ten years.
And then we pulled them down.

There's nothing left.
Ten years of killing left us with nothing
but a hunger for blood.
When we finally found ourselves
inside the walls of Troy,
we were like lions among cattle.
On the night before the city fell,
our army watched an eagle
fall upon a pregnant hare,
tear it open, spill the writhing young
in her blood on the ground.
We took this as an omen of our success.
And we showed as little mercy

when we tore open the walls of Troy.
The songs of the poets will say
that what we did was glorious.
Gods, let me forget it ever happened!

Chorus A.
This is not
how we expected to receive
the news of Troy's ruin.

Messenger.
The Greeks ruined themselves.
What treasure did we bring home from Troy?
These urns filled with the dust of our comrades.
The ones who survived come home
to wasted fields and wives
who no longer know them,
children who have grown into strangers.
Most of the men who made it out of Troy
sailed into a storm that sent rank after rank of waves
to batter the ships, as if the Trojan gods
had raised another army from the sea to send us down.
Our ships were scattered. Odysseus
and his crew were lost. Menelaus,
with Helen on board, the prize we fought for—
lost.

Chorus B. And Agamemnon?

Messenger.
His ship alone seemed to leap into the wind
as soon as the anchor was raised.
Like a hare running before hounds.
It ran ahead of the storm that scattered the rest of the Greeks.
His ship lies at anchor off the coast
at Nauplion[10]—
all that remains of the great army he led to Troy.

Chorus B (*urgently*). Tell Agamemnon—

(*The palace doors open. Clytemnestra rushes out, interrupting the Chorus. The Messenger hurries to make himself presentable.*)

Clytemnestra. You have news.

Messenger. Yes.

Clytemnestra. Troy has fallen.

Messenger. Yes.

Clytemnestra. And Agamemnon is coming home.

Messenger. Yes.

Clytemnestra. Say it.

Messenger. Troy has fallen and Agamemnon is coming home.

Clytemnestra.

(*To the Chorus.*)

This is just as I said it would be.
I knew exactly what the signs meant,
but you doubted me.
You doubted me because I'm a woman.
Well, now you've heard it from a man.
I knew this truth when it was
the faintest glimmer of light. I understood it.
I felt it moving inside me,
this great truth waiting to be born.
But you would only believe it
when it was put into a man's words.
For ten years—

(*She collects herself.*)

But it would be foolish on a day like this
to dwell on past hardships.

(*To the Messenger.*)

Tell Agamemnon to come quickly.
Now that he's done with Troy, Argos needs him.
He'll find everything in order.
Not that I can claim he'll find me exactly as he left me—
who can say that after ten years?—
but my heart is still the same. I haven't forgotten.
Tell him to come.

(*The Messenger hesitates.*)

What are you waiting for? Go.
Tell Agamemnon to come.

(*Exit Messenger. Clytemnestra returns to the palace and the doors close behind her.*)

(*During this long choral ode, which can be accompanied by dance, the blood-red carpet is laid out from the doors of the palace.*)

Chorus A.
Once a rich man brought
an orphaned lion cub into his home.
Its fur was soft and golden.
It curled and slept
beside the man's children.
It licked their faces,
tasting the salt of their skin,
and ate from their hands,
its low purr

like the rasp of a saw
starting a cut.

Chorus B.
There was still a wilderness in its mind.
It grew heraldic and insatiable,
its black mouth a drawer of knives.
It fell on the children first,
the taste of blood
stronger than affection.
The man and his wife died next,
rushing in on their children's slaughter.
And bursting from the house,
the lion ran like fire across the fields,
sowing them with blood,
slaughtering the shepherd
and his sheep,
the woman bringing water from the well,
the farmer working in his field,
the traveler on the road.

Chorus C.
Where did it start, this thirst for blood,
this hunger that devours the house of Atreus?
There were two brothers,
sons of Pelops who ruled in Argos,
who built this house,
and set two lions above the door.
Both brothers, equal
in strength and daring,
wanted to rule,
but Thyestes sat upon his father's throne.

Chorus A.
Like Tantalus,[11] his grandfather,
the gods gave Atreus a hunger.

He hungered for power,
and watched it slip into his brother's hands.
He watched his brother feast on his authority,
on the power he would pass to his sons,
while the sons of Atreus starved.
This hunger consumed him.
There was nothing left of him
but the beast that raged inside his mind.
Atreus butchered his brother's sons,
carved them into meat for their father's table,
and Thyestes, unsuspecting,
feasted on his children's flesh—
a crime that earned him banishment.

Chorus B.
But Thyestes in exile fathered
another son, Aegisthus.
Aegisthus might have been born motherless,
from the incestuous hatred of Atreus and Thyestes.[12]
Aegisthus was not a man.
He was a consequence.
A blade forged to strike back at Atreus.
He had no other purpose,
and when he had fulfilled it,
and Atreus was dead,
he could not hold the throne of Argos
long against the might of Atreus's son
Agamemnon.
So Aegisthus waits,
hungering still,
growing fat on Agamemnon's absence.

Chorus (*unison*). Helen![13]

Chorus C.
It was Helen who brought
this last misfortune down,

and involved the whole of Greece
in the curse on Agamemnon's house.
She was the lion,
the fire that spread across Greece.
She was the lust and the hunger,
and the madness that stole men's minds
and sent them rushing into war.
She brought Europe and Asia together
in a murderous embrace.

(*The music and dance segue into a procession for the entrance of Agamemnon. Agamemnon enters, accompanied by dancers. Cassandra follows.*)

Chorus and Dancers (*unison*). Agamemnon!

Agamemnon.
People of Argos!
To the gods of Argos first, I give my thanks
for delivering me safely home.
How good it is to be home
among a people at peace,
prepared to build the peaceful world
the war has won for us.
For ten long years we have fought
for the security of Greece,
for the sanctity of the bond
between husband and wife,
and of the bonds of hospitality
upon which all human society is based.
When Priam's son violated those bonds,
it was our sacred duty to ensure
that his act did not go unpunished.
Our indifference would have made us
complicit in the violation of those sacred obligations.
Our indifference would have been
an indifference to the gods of Argos

and to everything the Argives hold dear.
The gods have approved the justice of our cause.

Chorus and Dancers (*unison*). Agamemnon!

(*The palace doors open and Clytemnestra steps out.*)

Clytemnestra. Agamemnon. This is cause for celebration.

Agamemnon.
I've seen too much death to think
that celebration is what I've been spared for.
But the gods must be given their due.
It was the gods who brought us through
these ten years of war and delivered
Troy into our hands.
The gods unleashed the lion of Argos on Troy.
The gods bled Priam for taking Helen into his home.
Yes, by all means, let's thank the gods,
but then we should turn our attention
to the task of putting our own house in order.
I've been gone for too long.

Clytemnestra.
You have. And every hour
of your absence has clawed at my heart.
No one knew if you were alive or dead.
Rumors were carried like seeds on the wind.
Thorns began to take root
in the fallow field of your people's affection.
There were people who began to speculate
about what would happen
if the news came that you were dead.
There were some who looked upon your death
as an opportunity.
You know how speculations are shaped into plans,
and how plans begin to take on the substance of reality.

I had to send Orestes to our friend
Strophios in Phocis[14]
to put him out of reach of all the plots against him.
Your absence was like air and sunlight
to the ambitions of lesser men
accustomed to standing in your shade.
Little men sprouted up like weeds.
But now that you are home, all opposition will wither.

This carpet is laid for you, Agamemnon.
After everything you've done,
after everything you've accomplished—
it's not right that you should enter the house
like an ordinary mortal—
like some beggar in worn-out boots.

(*Gesturing to the Chorus.*)

Bring Agamemnon his crown!

(*One of the dancers brings a crown of golden laurels to the Chorus, who approaches to offer it to Agamemnon. He brushes it aside.*)

Agamemnon.
Stop.
Save your offerings for the gods.
A king, after all, is still a man. I have the example
of Priam to teach me the value of humility.
His feet never touched the ground.
He ruled god-like over Troy, but he learned
he could bleed like any man.
The war has changed things, Clytemnestra.
The men of Argos fought beside kings,
and learned that all men stand equal in the face of death.
Men who learned the lessons of equality at Troy
will never stand for tyranny at home.

Clytemnestra.
The men of Argos aren't the only ones
this war has changed.
The women of Argos, the ones you left behind—
the war has changed us, too.

Agamemnon.
Not all changes are equally desirable.

(*To the Chorus*.)

Take away this carpet.
A king can walk on the ground like other men.

Clytemnestra (*to the Chorus*).
Wait.

(*To Agamemnon.*)

Why do we fight, Agamemnon?
I wanted this to be a new beginning.
We've spent ten years married to each other's absence.
We can't keep looking past each other
at the people we've created to fill that absence.
We have to learn to see each other again.
I want to know you as I once knew you,
before the war came between us.
This carpet isn't laid out for a conquerer,
or a man who would make himself a tyrant—
it's laid out for the bridegroom coming home to his bride.

Agamemnon.
We're not as young as we once were, Clytemnestra.
We can't pretend our past lives were lived by someone else.

Clytemnestra. No. Of course not. But—

Agamemnon.
But these are things for a husband and wife
to discuss in private, not in front of strangers.

Clytemnestra.
Then come inside.
This is all I want, Agamemnon.
I only want us to be together.
I only want to be a wife to you again.
I wove this carpet with my own hands
through ten years of longing for you.
Each thread was spun from my own heart,
each pass of the shuttle through the loom
bound me closer in affection to the husband
I dreamed would one day come to me again.
What I have laid before you is my life, Agamemnon.

(*To the Chorus.*)

Take away the carpet.

(*The Chorus moves to roll up the carpet.*)

Agamemnon.

(*To the Chorus.*)

Stop. Leave it.

(*To Clytemnestra.*)

My mind is still at war.

(*Clytemnestra holds out her hand to him.*)

Clytemnestra. I'm not your enemy, Agamemnon.

(*While Agamemnon speaks the following, Clytemnestra bends down and removes his boots, leaving them side by side.*)

Agamemnon.
I look at my own house, and I see Troy.
I look at this carpet,
and I see the battlefield soaked with blood.
I see my daughter Iphigeneia.
My eyes have filled up with everything they've seen,
and they can't hold anything more.
I've seen more death than life.
I see Achilles dragging Hector's bloody corpse
around the walls of Troy,
as if he were trying to outrun
the consequences of his actions.
Finding that he was still bound to them.
I feel now as if I'm dragging my own corpse behind me.

Clytemnestra. (*Stands up and offers him her hand again.*) Let me help you.

Agamemnon.
Wait a moment.

(*He goes and takes Cassandra by the hand and leads her to the Chorus.*)

This is Cassandra, Priam's daughter.
Take care of her.
She's suffered more than all of us.

(*Chorus C takes Cassandra's hand. Agamemnon steps onto the carpet.*)

(*To himself, looking at the carpet.*)

This is all such a waste.

(*Agamemnon walks on the carpet into the palace. Clytemnestra follows, *walking beside the carpet. She closes the palace doors behind her. Cassandra stands staring at Agamemnon's empty boots.*)

Chorus C.
That went about as well as could be expected.

(*To Cassandra.*)

What's wrong? You look as if you'd seen a ghost.

(*The palace doors open again. Clytemnestra stands in the doorway.*)

Clytemnestra.
Cassandra.

(*Cassandra starts, and hides behind the members of the Chorus. Clytemnestra approaches and speaks gently.*)

Cassandra? Let me see you.

(*Cassandra hesitantly steps out from behind the Chorus. She sings wordlessly, almost inaudibly, to herself. Clytemnestra studies her.*)

You're the age my Iphigeneia would have been.
You might have been sisters.
Poor thing. Come with me into the house.

(*She reaches out her hand to Cassandra, who shrinks from her.*)

Do you understand?

(*To the Chorus.*)

I don't think she understands what I'm saying.
There's something wild about her.

(*To Cassandra, louder and slower.*)

Won't you come inside?

(*Cassandra hides behind the Chorus again. Clytemnestra impatiently addresses the Chorus.*)

I can't stand here all day. I have things to do.
Send her in when she's ready to come.

(*Clytemnestra turns, kicks aside the carpet, and re-enters the palace. The carpet is drawn into the palace behind her. The doors close. Cassandra wanders to center stage.*)

Cassandra. Apollo!

Chorus C. (*Comfortingly.*) Hush.

Cassandra. Apollo!

Chorus A. Poor girl. Hush.

Cassandra.
Apollo!
Look what you've done!
My voice was never my own.
I was your songbird, and you were my cage.
I hated you for what you had done to me.
And because I was what you had made me,
I hated myself.
I looked inside myself,
to see if something else was there,
and all I saw was your reflection.

Apollo!
You filled me with nightmares.
I lived among ruins. I moved among the dead.
The light you placed before me cast
the shadows of future things across my mind.

You buried me alive
inside myself,
inside this knowledge you gave me,
these self-obliterating visions.

Apollo!
You filled me with nightmares,
and I watched each of them born,
torn from the womb of my prophecy—
bloody, stillborn things.
Where are you now, Apollo?
You filled me and then withdrew.
You made me the mother of my own destruction.

(*Approaching Agamemnon's boots, she reaches out as if to touch someone standing there.*)

I see things, but my hand passes through them.
There's nothing that I can move or change.

(*Cassandra approaches the Chorus, slowly reaching out her hand to touch them. She's surprised to find that the Chorus members are real and solid.*)

Chorus B. What happened to you?

Cassandra.
Apollo.
I refused him my body, so he took my mind.
He filled me with truths no one would believe.
It was as good as not having a voice at all.
My words became the shadows of invisible things.
I watched my brothers step out into the shadow of their own deaths—
I told Coroebus[15] how he would die,
stabbed through the heart as he tried to save me.
The last thing on earth he saw was Ajax forcing
himself upon me in Athena's temple—

Ajax who would die in madness for what he had done.
I saw how they all would die,
but men prefer blindness to that kind of sight.

At least there's no one left to avenge my death.
My father and my brothers are all dead—
my sisters, too, for all I know.
My death doesn't have to mean anything.
Death only means something to the ones left behind.
It becomes an occasion. It becomes a cause.
The dead no longer belong to themselves.
But my death will be different.
I've always belonged to Apollo—
my dreams were Apollo's thoughts,
my mouth spoke Apollo's words.
Death will be the only thing that has ever been mine.

(*Cassandra turns and walks toward the palace doors. She hesitates.*)

This house is a beast that devours its young.
I can hear their cries, I can see
the blood poured out on the hearth.

Chorus C.
It's only the ritual
for Agamemnon's safe return.

Cassandra.
It's like the breath from an open grave—
the smell of death, the stink of corruption.

Chorus C.
It's only the incense
burned for the ritual.

Cassandra.
I see nothing now.

Nothing but darkness.
It's almost a relief.

(*The doors open, Cassandra steps inside, and they close behind her. The Chorus watches her go. As the doors are closing, Chorus C rushes up to them, but she is shut out. She turns away from the closed doors.*)

Chorus C. When will we sing a new song?

(*A soft drumbeat, like a pulse, begins, and gradually increases in volume and intensity throughout the following.*)

Chorus A.
For ten years, the beat of doom has sounded in our ears,
and death has spread its shadow over Greece.

Chorus C. When will we sing a new song?

Chorus B.
The soldier's broken body remembers the war.
The widow's broken heart remembers the war.

Chorus C. When will we sing a new song?

Agamemnon (*from inside the palace*). Murder!

Chorus A. Do something! Quick! Call out the army!

Chorus B.
And have them raise a bloodier general to rule in Agamemnon's place?
Rally the people of Argos!

This is our chance to free ourselves from the rule of tyrants
and take power into our own hands.

Agamemnon. Murder!

Chorus A.
The people?
And be ruled by a thousand tyrants instead of one?

Chorus B.
Do something!
There may never be another chance like this.

Chorus C (*calling out*).
Argives!
Come to the palace!
They're killing Agamemnon!

(*The dancers enter to the frantic pulse of the drumbeats.*)

Agamemnon. Murder![16]

(*The drumbeats stop. A moment of silence, then confusion. No one knows what to do or who's in charge. In the midst of this confusion, Clytemnestra appears on the roof of the palace.*)

Clytemnestra.
People of Argos!
The day of your liberation has come.
Agamemnon is dead.

Chorus A. Murderer!

Clytemnestra.
This was not murder.
This was your liberation.
I did this to free the people of Argos.
Agamemnon was the murderer. He murdered his own daughter.
He led thousands of men to their deaths.
For what?
What was gained with so much blood?
Nothing.

Ashes.
Poets will do their best
to fill these senseless deaths with meaning,
but their stories are for a generation not yet born,
for a generation far removed from the pain of actual loss.
For us there must be action, not words.

Chorus A. Murderer!

Chorus C. Listen!

Clytemnestra.
Agamemnon should have died at Troy.
He should have died before that, at Aulis,
before he had a chance to sacrifice his daughter,
before the wind rose to carry so many other men to their deaths.
A hundred times he should have died before this.
His one death would have saved thousands.

Chorus C. She's right. Listen to her.

Chorus A.
She's a murderer.

(*To Clytemnestra.*)

Open the doors!
If you did this for the people,
show the people what you've done.

Clytemnestra. Open the doors!

(*The palace doors open. Agamemnon is lying dead on platform inside the palace. Cassandra lies dead at the foot of the platform.*)

Clytemnestra.
Look at him!

Caught in the net
he fashioned for himself
with his own crimes.
He came home with a girl young enough
to be the daughter he killed,
a girl as young as I was when I became his wife.
Did he think he could replace what he had lost?
Did he think he could pretend
the last ten years never happened?
Even a king could not escape the snares
he set for himself, the blade
his own cruelty placed into my hand.
Agamemnon caught himself
in the wide net he cast to capture Troy.

You witnessed the scene he made over the carpet—
how he demanded it be taken away,
how I yielded,
how he ordered it to stay.
He only wanted to make me yield.
Nothing gave him pleasure unless it demonstrated his power.

(*Aegisthus emerges from shadows inside the palace and steps outside.*)

Chorus B.
Here's your accomplice,
Aegisthus.

(*To Aegisthus.*)

What do you want?

Aegisthus.
Justice.
That's all I've ever wanted.
This is what justice looks like.
If you want justice to be more than a word,

more than a dream that belongs to a future that never comes,
there has to be blood.
Some of you wanted a revolution.
This is what your revolution looks like.
If you want to change the world,
there has to be blood.

Chorus C. Then give us blood.

(*Improvised shouts from the crowd, demanding Aegisthus's blood. The mood is revolutionary. Armed guards emerge from the wings.*)

Aegisthus.
Hasn't my family given enough?
Have you forgotten my brothers,
the children Atreus butchered?
We've purchased Argos with our blood.

Chorus A.
You've purchased nothing but our hatred.
You've bled Agamemnon,
and now you mean to bleed his people dry.

Aegisthus.
You're my people now.
You'll soon learn to recognize your master.

(*The guards move in to clash with the crowd.*)

Clytemnestra.
Stop!

(*The action below is suspended.*)

There's been enough killing.
Agamemnon's death was a necessary sacrifice.
But it ends here.

(*Aegisthus slips into the palace, and the doors close. A moment later, he appears on the palace roof beside Clytemnestra. She places on his head the crown that Agamemnon had earlier refused.*)

The war is over.

(*Clytemnestra and Aegisthus exit. The guards move in and clash with the protesters. Banners are raised. Political graffiti accumulates on the walls of the palace. Choreographed scenes of protest. Gradually, the stage clears. A little girl, the young Electra, emerges from the dispersing crowd and crosses to Agamemnon's boots. She picks them up and hugs them. Suddenly afraid, she puts them down again and runs to the palace. She opens the doors and goes inside.[17] The doors close. The stage is briefly empty, except for the boots, which serve as a "headstone" for Agamemnon's grave in the following scene.*

Orestes enters, alone, barefoot.)

Orestes.[18]
So this is Argos.
This is what Argos has become:
this dung heap.
Not as I remember it,
not as I've dreamed of it all these years.
On one side the mountain, a huge gray mass,
and the deep fold of the gorge
slashing down into the greener landscape
below the city walls.
A landscape empty of humans,
but full of gods.
The mountain and the gorge were god and goddess,
and this citadel their mortal child.
That was the home I remembered,
the land I dreamed about every night in exile:
the land where I would be king
when my father closed his eyes after the gods

had given him a long and happy life.
Not this wasteland.

(*Electra emerges from the palace with an offering for Agamemnon's grave. Orestes hides as Electra crosses to the grave. The grave, with the boots as a "headstone" should be simple, perhaps only indicated by a rectangle of light.*)

Electra.
What a mess.

(*She picks up Agamemnon's boots.*)

I wanted to forgive you.
I imagined you coming home,
not the same man who killed my sister,
but a man who needed forgiveness.
That was something I could have given you.

(*Orestes makes a sound, and Electra is startled. She looks toward where Orestes is hiding.*)[19]

Who's there?
Come out where I can see you.

(*Orestes comes out of hiding, and steps toward her.*)

Stay where you are.

Orestes. Or what? You'll throw those boots at me?

Electra. Who are you?

Orestes (*evasively*). Is this the grave of Agamemnon?

Electra. Yes.

(*Orestes approaches the grave to make an offering of a lock of his hair. Electra cautiously makes way for him, watching him closely as he makes the offering. When he's done, he addresses her again.*)

Orestes.
I was wondering about those boots.
Would you mind if I tried them on?
I've been walking so long I've worn through my soles.

(*She allows him to approach. She studies his face, there may be a glimmer of recognition.*)

Electra. I had a brother who would have been about your age.

(*She hands him the boots. They sit side by side, and she helps him into the boots.*)

Orestes. What happened to him?

Electra. My mother sent him away.

Orestes. Do you remember him at all?

Electra. No.

(*She finishes tying up the boots.*)

There. How's that?

Orestes. A perfect fit.

(*They stand and face each other. A glimmer of recognition. He turns away and steps over to the palace doors, looking at the graffiti and debris from the protests.*)

What happened here?

Electra.
The end of the world.
This is what there is left.
It's as if a fire consumed the world,
the earth's holocaust,
and all that could be salvaged from the flames
were our hatreds.
Everything else was burned down to ash,
but the fire forged hatred
into something harder and stronger.
Look at this.
We're trying to rebuild the world
with nothing but grief and hatred.
No wonder it keeps falling apart.
But why am I telling you this?
Who are you?

Orestes.
I was sent here by a god.
He has work for me to do here.
Electra. But you still haven't told me who you are.

Orestes.
You know who I am.
Electra—

(*She recognizes him, but the Chorus enters and comes between them.*)

Chorus A.[20]
We come to honor the dead.
Ten years of war,
years of barren homecomings,
have brought us nothing but grief.
We fill our empty lives with mourning—
like the Danaids,[21] pouring water
into urns that can never be filled,
that drain away in perpetual weeping.

Chorus B.
We still weep for the sons of Thyestes,
dead at their father's table—
a tale too bitter for the tongue to tell.

Chorus C.
We still weep for Iphigeneia,
blameless Iphigeneia, pure and lovely
as the white anemone
flowering in some high and windy place.
Iphigeneia plucked from life,
Iphigeneia whose blood
flowed from the wounds
of all the Greeks who fell at Troy.

Chorus A.
We still weep for a great king,
a mighty warrior—
though his murderers have made it
a crime to speak his name.

Chorus B.
History is written in blood.
Blood is the gift each generation
passes on to the next.
Each father hands his son
a blood-stained sword, and says:
Take this in remembrance of me.
It never ends, this communion
of the living with the dead.
Because a hundred, or a thousand,
or ten thousand years ago,
one of my people
threw a stone at one of yours,
today we slash each other with swords.

Chorus C.
What can women do but mourn?
The generations pass through us,
from death to death,
and leave us empty.
Broken urns,
ashes
scattered to the wind.

(*Orestes approaches the grave and addresses his dead father.*)

Orestes.
You are not dead as long as there is still life in me.
We are not meant to measure out our lives
by our body's brief span:
this flesh is too small a vessel to contain us.
There is no end and no beginning.

Chorus A.
You're a stranger here,
but you make offerings to the dead of Argos.

Orestes.
Argos was the land of my fathers,
but most of my life has passed in exile.
I haven't seen this place in many years,
and then it was not as I see it now.

Chorus B.
We're all exiles here.
Our home is in the past.

Chorus C.
This was once a land of heroes:
the land of Perseus,

who founded this citadel of Mycenae,
and of Herakles,
who ruled over Tiryns to the south—
and of Agamemnon,
who ruled over all the lands from here to the sea,
whose power extended across the sea
to the blood-black plain of Troy.
Agamemnon led to Troy
the greatest force the world has known
or will ever know again:
no other army will boast an Ajax,
a Diomedes,
an Odysseus,
an Achilles.
Agamemnon led them all—
and the men of Argos were the heart
and the sinew of the Greek army.

(*Beat.*)
Chorus A.
Now all of that is gone.
The strength of Argos was spent at Troy.
The land of Perseus and Herakles
and Agamemnon
is ruled by Aegisthus,
a nobody,
a king of shadows.
In former times, our kings made us stronger—
their might was measured
by the strength of the Argive people,
by the richness of our flocks and fields.
But now carrion
pick the flesh from our bones,
and Aegisthus fattens himself on our remains.

(*Electra takes Orestes aside while the dancers and Chorus perform a ritual of mourning.*)

Electra (*urgently, to Orestes*). Why have you come back?

Orestes.
I've had no peace since I learned of my father's death.
The thoughts swarm in my head like stinging bees.
If I sleep at all, I find myself drowning in a pool of blood—
the same thing every night. My dreams coagulate.
At last, I sought the counsel of the god at Delphi—
Apollo the healer—who saw that my father's murder
was the cause of this illness that destroys my peace.
The god himself has shown me what I have to do.

(*He takes a knife from his belt.*)

It is my father's ghost who haunts my mind,
demanding the blood of his murderers.
I will give him their blood.
I hold this knife, but it is my father who raises his hand.
When I drive this blade into that woman's faithless heart,
it is my father who trades blow for blow,
Agamemnon himself who strikes back where he has been struck.
Apollo assures me of this:
I will bear no guilt for these deaths.
This is what the god himself has sent me here to do—
to commit this blameless murder.

Electra (*taking the knife from Orestes*).
If I had the strength—
if the god had sent me—
I would do the same.
Do you know how she hates us,
you and me,
her own children?
No—not her children.
She had only one child.
Iphigeneia.
You and I, Orestes,

are what remains
of a life that she
no longer thinks of as hers.
The woman who was our mother—
you won't find her here.
You'll find a thing of stone.

Chorus A.
Her nights are broken with terror.
She's afraid of sleep,
afraid of some terror
that takes shape in the darkness
and haunts her dreams.

Electra.
She dreams she's suffering
the pangs of childbirth.
She feels her body split open,
like an earthquake
opening a great rent in the ground.
But she bears no human child.

Chorus A.
What prodigy awakes
to chase her from her sleep?
Something terrible rises
from the abyss of her dreams.

Electra.
She dreams a snake,
uncoiling from her body,
raising its head to strike,
baring its bloody fangs.
She nurses the snake at her breast,
and her blood curdles the milk,
and she feels a coldness in her heart.

Chorus A.
This is why she orders
the torches to burn all night—
to chase this terror from her mind.
This is why she sends us here with offerings
to appease the restless dead.

Orestes. Apollo has sent her prophetic dreams.

Chorus A (*softly*). Agamemnon!

Chorus B, C, Dancers. Agamemnon!

Orestes.
Soon the snake she dreamed
will change its skin
and come to her in its true shape,
more terrible than she imagined.

Chorus.

(*Still softly.*)

Agamemnon!

(*Louder.*)

Agamemnon!

(*Louder.*)

Agamemnon!

(*Electra sees Aegisthus approaching with guards.*)

Electra (*to Orestes, handing him the knife*). Aegisthus.

(*Orestes blends in with the Chorus as Aegisthus approaches.*)

Aegisthus.
Though his body lies in the ground,
the name of Agamemnon is still powerful.
They love his memory
more than they loved the man.

Electra (*approaching Aegisthus*).
You murdered his faults,
but you left an ideal to rally them.

Aegisthus.
And they have you—
Agamemnon's daughter.

Electra. Why haven't you had me killed?

Aegisthus. We're too much alike, you and I.

Electra. I'm nothing like you.

Aegisthus.
We were both shaped by things
that happened before we were born.
We were both replacements—
I for my dead brothers, the ones Atreus killed,
and you for Iphigeneia.
I know you.

Electra.
You don't know me.
You know nothing about me.

Aegisthus.
We're like tortoises, you and I,
carrying our houses on our backs.

We both carry the house of Atreus on our backs.
We're born into our histories,
and they harden around us like a shell.

Electra.
We're stained with blood—
and the stain is spreading.
I only want to be washed clean.

Aegisthus.
That's impossible.
The only way forward is through blood.

Electra.
When you killed Atreus,
did it make good the deaths of your brothers?
Was Agamemnon's death
payment for the death of Iphigeneia?
Was it a fair exchange?
Or was it just more waste of life?

(*Orestes approaches.*)

Aegisthus. It was justice.

Electra.
It was retribution.
There's a difference.

Aegisthus.
It's the difference of a word.
The facts are the same.

(*To the guards.*)

Take the girl away.
Her presence here incites the crowd.

(*The guards take Electra away. Now Aegisthus notices Orestes.*)

What is it?

Orestes.
I come with news from Phocis.[22]
I'm afraid that what I have to say
will come as a heavy blow
to the mother of Orestes.

Aegisthus.
Then let the blow fall on me first.
What is your news?
(*Orestes draws his knife. The Chorus closes around Orestes and Aegisthus, screening the audience from what happens. Aegisthus calls out, then falls. The Chorus moves to reveal Aegisthus's body. Orestes sheathes his knife, drags Aegisthus's body offstage, and goes up to pound on the door of the palace. While Orestes is doing this, the Chorus speaks.*)

Chorus A.
The earth[23] was first—
first of the gods, quickening
in the womb of the void,
born in a spasm of light,
murdering the emptiness
from which she came.
Mother of gods and men,
all things claim kinship through her—
the farmer and his field
and the ox who draws his plow,
the storm and the sailor,
the lioness and her prey.
The struggle for life
was the earth's only law.

Chorus B.
From Earth came

the generations of sky-dwelling gods—
Ouranos, Kronos, Zeus—[24]
and the ancient powers of darkness,
the Furies,
who sprang to life
from drops of blood
when Kronos cut his father from the sky.
Poor little human,
coming late to his place
among Earth's children,
found the world crowded with powers.
Huge shadows pressed him on every side—
Fear and Strife,
and all the Night's immortal children.

Orestes.

(*He pounds on the palace doors.*)

Open the door!
I've come with news of Orestes.

Chorus B. He was frightened, short-lived, and alone.

(*The palace doors open, revealing Clytemnestra.*)

Clytemnestra (*gripping Orestes's arm*). Where is Orestes?

Orestes.
He lies
dead at Delphi.

Clytemnestra.
How? How did he die?

Orestes.
In the games at Delphi.[25]

There was an accident—
the axle shattered, Orestes
thrown from the chariot,
his—

Clytemnestra. Yes?

Orestes.
His body broken
beyond recognition.
His own mother would not know him.

Clytemnestra.
I was his mother.

(*Orestes watches her for a sign of recognition. Nothing. She is impatient.*)

Has he been given a proper burial?

Orestes. Yes. At Delphi.

Cytemnestra.
Good.
Then everything has been done
that must be done.
You have discharged your obligation.
The gods are satisfied.

Orestes. The gods are not satisfied.

Clytemnestra. What did you say?

Orestes.
The gods will not be satisfied
until I do what I've come here to do.

Clytemnestra.
You've done that.
Is there something more?

Orestes.
No.
There's nothing.
No grief, no remorse.
I come here a stranger,
reporting the death of a stranger.
I thought I might make you feel something.

(*Drawing his knife.*)

But there's only one way to make you feel.

Clytemnestra.
Orestes?

(*She approaches him, but he holds her off with his knife.*)

My poor child.
You're home now.
Put down the knife, Orestes,
and let me hold you.
Let me welcome you home.

Orestes. As you welcomed home my father?

Clytemnestra.
I'm not the one
who murdered my own children.

Orestes.
You were relieved
when you thought I was dead.

Clytemnestra.
Not relieved, Orestes.
I've lost other children before you.
Iphigeneia's loss has left me numb to other loss.

Orestes.
I never knew Iphigeneia.
I grew up thinking Iphigeneia
was the name of my misfortune.

Clytemnestra. She was an innocent girl.

Orestes. And you made her into a guilty cause.

Clytemnestra.
The guilt was Agamemnon's.
He killed his daughter.
He dragged the Greeks into a war,
and stained even his victory with outrage.
He came home from Troy
with another woman,
the daughter of Priam—
defeated, but no less proud
in her father's royal blood.
Their child would have taken your place
as she had taken mine.

Orestes.
I was my father's first-born son.
While he still lived, my place was secure.

Clytemnestra. And will be now.

Orestes. Yes. I've seen to that. Aegisthus is dead.

Clytemnestra.
Let it end there, Orestes.

We have years ahead of us,
you and I,
to remember the bond between us.
Don't steal the future from us
in anger for what is past.
You've come so close, Orestes.
Put down the knife, and come to me.

Orestes. So you can send me after my father?

Clytemnestra. So I can comfort you.

Orestes.
Electra has shown me
what a comfort you are to your children.
She's like a ghost haunting Agamemnon's grave,
like some posthumous child risen from his ashes.
She's as gaunt as smoke.
She still had his old boots,
still covered with the dust of Troy.

Clytemnestra.
If Agamemnon had lived,
he would have made her
Cassandra's slave.
His son with Cassandra
would have taken your place.
Everything I did, I did for you.

Orestes.
You did it for yourself.
You've never done anything
for anyone but yourself.

Clytemnestra.
How can you say that
to a woman who's borne children?

I gave my body to you.
I carried you under my heart.
I went through the pangs of childbirth for you—
how can you possibly say I've done nothing for you?

(*Orestes advances with the knife.*)

You're the snake.
In my dream.
You're the snake I nursed.
It's your venom that freezes my heart.

Orestes.
You have this much conscience at least—
for your guilt to father such a dream.

Clytemnestra.
Do this, Orestes,
and you unleash the hounds
of a mother's curse.

(*Orestes pulls Clytemnestra into the palace. The doors close. Clytemnestra screams offstage.*)

Chorus A. What's happening?

Chorus B. What have I done?

Chorus C. I thought justice—

Chorus A. I thought justice would be done.

(*The palace doors open, revealing Clytemnestra dead on the platform where earlier Agamemnon's body lay. All around her, the dancers lie in blood-red garments, their heads are covered so they seem to form a billowing sea of blood rather than distinct individuals. Orestes, with blood on his hands, steps forward.*)

Orestes.
It's done.
She's been caught in the same net
that snared my father.
The same bloody trail she laid for him
has led her back to her own end.
(*Looking around at the silent Chorus members.*)

You know I had to do this.
To avenge my father.
To throw off the tyranny
that sat heavy on Argos.
Why won't you speak to me now?
This was for Argos,
this blood on my hands—

Chorus B. Why is there blood on my hands?

(*Red light on his outstretched hands.*)

Chorus C. Why is darkness rising from the earth to cover me?

(*Raises a black hood to cover her head.*)

Chorus B. What is happening to me?

(*The Chorus members raise black hoods over their heads. As Orestes approaches each Chorus member, he or she turns away from him. The dancers rise from around Clytemnestra's body and surge out of the palace to surround Orestes.*)

Act II

(*The scene is changed to Delphi. Enter Pythia; or she could speak as a voice-over, since she is the mysterious voice of the Delphic oracle. While Pythia speaks, the Furies lie sleeping around the altar of Apollo, twitching and whimpering like sleeping dogs. Orestes stands at the altar.*)

Pythia.[26]
This is Delphi:
the center of the world,
birth-scar of the Earth itself,
oldest and holiest.
All human fates are spun from this center.
First Earth herself
was worshipped here,
and wilderness,
and the elemental powers.
Then Earth yielded her place
to Themis,
goddess of order,
who first gave men the impulse
to seek out others of their kind,
to form tribes
joined by the interests of common blood.
And finally now Apollo
keeps his temple here,
bright marble above the cave
where men once worshipped Earth in darkness.
Here Apollo found a monstrous serpent,
the Python, rising in fury from its cave
like Earth's own flickering tongue.
Only Apollo could slay this serpent,

and claim the navel of the Earth for Zeus.
Apollo, who civilizes men,
who puts great thoughts into their minds,
who finally makes them more than beasts.
Here Apollo translates
the mind of Zeus into human thoughts,
and I shape those thoughts into speech.

But here's a thing I can't explain—
this stranger with blood on his hands,
and these women—
no, not women—
this pack of fiends
crowded around the altar of the god.
They came like hell hounds
on the scent of blood—
and now they sleep,
twitching like dogs
still running in their dreams.

(*Exit Pythia. Enter Apollo.*)

Apollo.

(*To Orestes.*)

I've brought you this far, Orestes.
I won't abandon you.
These curses that follow you—
they can be laid to rest.
Now they are only sleeping,
but you can make them change.
They are curses now, deformed,
the shape of an ancient hatred,
but you can change them into blessings.

Orestes. But how?

Apollo.
Make your way to Athens.
These creatures will follow you there.
Athena has the power to do the rest.

(*Exit Apollo, leading Orestes. Enter the Ghost of Clytemnestra. Alternately, she may rise from among the sleeping Furies, or appear as a projection.*)

Clytemnestra.
Sleeping?
How can you lie there
and let your quarry go to ground?
He can't wash my blood
so easily from his hands.
My blood is his blood.
His heart is stained with it.
Get up! Clytemnestra demands it—
the one who raised you from the earth.
Go after him, curses!

(*The Furies begin to wake.*)

Get up, you nest of snakes!
Shed this useless skin of dreams.
Get up, you children of blood!

(*The Furies rise. Apollo re-enters. Clytemnestra exits/disappears.*)

Apollo. Who brought this pollution into my temple?

Chorus A.
You invited us yourself,
when you moved Orestes's hand
against his mother
and offered him refuge here.
We are your elders, Apollo.

Our power is as strong
and ancient as the earth—
we were old before your father Zeus
took possession of the sky.
Before your temple rose
upon this patch of rocky ground,
the entire earth was ours.
We have a right to assert our claim.

Apollo. Out! You have no business with me now.

Chorus B.
Our business is with Orestes.
He summoned us.
We rose from the drops of mother's blood
he spilled upon the earth.
He made us.
We are his consequences.

Apollo.
What did he do?
He took revenge
on his father's murderer.

Chorus C. He killed his mother.

Apollo. And Clytemnestra killed her husband.

Chorus A.
Agamemnon took his daughter's life.
His own blood ran in Iphigeneia's veins.
But the blood that Clytemnestra spilled
was not her own.
A husband's isn't kindred blood.

Apollo.
But it was the blood she bound herself to

when she made her marriage vows.
Orestes was the curse she laid upon herself
when she broke those vows.

Chorus B.
Orestes owes his life to her.
She made him, she brought him into the world.
When he killed her, he erased himself.

Apollo.
He made himself.
While she lived,
there was a part of Orestes
that was not his own.

Chorus C. Now he belongs to us.

Apollo.
Go!
I've sent Orestes to Athens,
to seek a judgment from Athena.

Chorus A. Even there he won't escape us.

Apollo.
He's under my protection.
Follow if you will—
you'll never touch him.

(*Exit Apollo. A choral dance of the Furies can indicate the shift of scene from Delphi to Athens,[27] where Orestes enters.*)

Orestes. Athena!

Chorus.
There's no escape
from your mother's curse.

Orestes. Athena!

Chorus.
Your mother's blood
has bound you to us.

Orestes. Athena!

Chorus A.
Blood is stronger.
You reach out your hands
to a younger power—
motherless,
sitting high in her temple
that reason built,
thinking she can rule the earth
with her geometry.
There are deeper things.
There are older things—
passions—compulsions—terrors—
anger—guilt—
burning, blinding, irrational hatreds.
Men build a world of right angles
to worship Athena,
but your hearts are twisted things,
and belong to us.

Chorus B.
We are older than the gods
in temples that humans built
with guilt-stained hands.
Every block of stone they raise
is a prayer for undeserved forgiveness.
Those same hands
are raised in anger,
cast stones that draw blood—
and we dwell in the blood men spill,

as the gods dwell in their temples of stone.
Temples rise and fall
with the tide of men's devotion,
but blood flows—
steady, strong, outlasting—
from mother to son,
from generation to generation.

Orestes. Athena!

(*Enter Athena, with attendants.*)

Athena.
Who are you?
You inhuman shapes—what are you?
What brings you here?
And you, stranger—what is your business here?

Chorus B.
We are the Furies, Night's immortal children,
curses summoned from the darkest places of the earth.

Orestes.
Orestes, son of Agamemnon.
Apollo sent me here to reclaim my innocence.

Chorus C.
Innocence?
The man killed his own mother.

Orestes. I was following the commands of Apollo.

Athena.
Enough!
I won't have the justice of the street
govern the city of Athens.
I won't have these acts of blood multiply

as they have in Argos,
and have the city die by its own hand.
Athens is a city of laws.
Choose twelve Athenian men by lot—
twelve impartial men
to decide this stranger's guilt or innocence.[28]

(*The jury is assembled.*)

Chorus C.
What is it that keeps the world
from falling apart?
Is it human self-restraint,
or their devotion to the gods?
No—
one thing keeps man in his place,
tames him,
makes him dream more than he dares:
fear.
Fear guards over all of his actions.
Fear is what makes men walk the narrow path
they call righteousness.

Athena.
Silence!
The jury is assembled.
This trial is called to order.

This man, Orestes, has—
by his own admission—
committed the crime of matricide.
He claims that the act was justified,
and done at Apollo's command.
This is what you are to determine—
shall he be exonerated, free from guilt,
or handed over to the powers assembled here
for punishment.

Chorus A.
The man has confessed.
His hands are stained with his mother's blood.

Orestes.
I was following the orders of the god
Apollo, who demanded justice
for my father's murder.
I was the instrument of that justice,
which came from the god.

(*To the Chorus.*)

If justice is what you are after,
where were you when Agamemnon was murdered?

Chorus B.
We punish crimes of blood.
There was no blood shared between
Clytemnestra and Agamemnon.

Orestes.
There was a bond sworn before the gods.
Do I belong more to my mother than she belonged to him?

Chorus C.
She belonged to him by convention.
You belong to her by blood.

Orestes.
Apollo, I am here by your command.
Help me answer this charge!

(*Enter Apollo.*)

Apollo.
The whole truth—

this is what I can offer you.
Not one man's truth, but the truth
of Zeus, whose prophet I am.
True: this man, Orestes, killed Clytemnestra—

Chorus. Guilty!

Apollo.
Abominations!
Go hide yourselves
in the dark recesses of the earth.
But you, good men of the jury,
hear me out.
This woman, Clytemnestra,
not only murdered her husband,
she assassinated the head of state—
a man who, by his position,
was a representative of Zeus on earth:
the source of law and of power for his people.
Not just murder, but treason was her crime.
From her act began the unraveling
of the Argive state.
Agamemnon gave his people
laws and victories,
brought home the spoils of Troy,
followed the commands of the gods,
laid down the foundations of future glory
for himself and for the Argive people.
The gods gave him every success—
and one woman dared to take it all away.
If a woman can with impunity do this to a king,
who will stop men from mounting Olympos
and throwing down the gods?
There is an order that must be preserved.
A man's devotion to that order
must be stronger than any other affection—
stronger even than the ties of blood.

Chorus A.
Without blood there is no life—
through it, through the bonds it forms,
life is passed from mother to child:
and so it has been from the beginning.
Orestes's crime was a crime against life itself.

Apollo.
Your thoughts are so earthbound
that you think only of bodies—
vessels of blood poured one into the next,
and human history nothing
but a blind staggering from one coupling to another.
As if men belonged only to their bodies,
and not to the gods.
I will tell you this:
a woman is not the parent of her child,
but only the field a man plants with his seed.
It is the man who gives life
its beginning and its end.
The end of a man's life, his purpose,
is to find his place in the order of things,
to serve that order—
to be a son second and a citizen first.
As a member of the state,
Orestes belonged more to Agamemnon
than to his mother.
As the heir to his father's authority
as the head of state,
he had an obligation to punish treason
with death.
It makes no difference that the traitor
was his own mother.
Justice makes no such distinctions.

Chorus B.
This is not what I call justice.

Orestes owes his life to her.
He was knit together from her flesh
and carried under her heart.
If the bond between a mother
and her child is broken,
what is there to keep
the entire world from dissolving?
Clytemnestra held her children in her arms,
felt them moving inside her own body:
they were a part of her
before they were a part of anything else.

Apollo.
There is something greater than a mother's love—
the love of country.
Countless women of Greece
were filled with this love
when they sent their sons and husbands
with Agamemnon to fight for Greece.
They sacrificed what was most dear to them as mothers
for what was even dearer to them as Greeks—
Greece itself.
Iphigeneia herself felt this
when she gave her life for Greece.
Clytemnestra alone was unwilling to accept the sacrifice.
Here I rest my case.

Chorus C.
This god may change men's minds,
but the facts remain the same.
Sons will still come
from their mothers' wombs
and feed at their mothers' breasts.
No jury can overturn the laws of nature.

Athena.
Silence!

(*Addressing the jury.*)

Citizens, men of Attica,
you have heard the case against this man,
and his defense.
Now you must judge.
For the first time, men have come together
to render judgment in a case of murder.
For the first time, justice shall be rendered
by the ballot and not by the sword.
Take care with the precedent you set.
It is not simply one man's fate you decide—
you decide for the ages how justice will be done.

(*Dance while the jury deliberates and casts its ballots.*)

Chorus A.
No ballot can bind us.
These upstart gods
seek to strip us of our power.
But we have outlasted generations of the gods.
One day nothing will be left of these gods
but the ideas they represent.
But we will survive.

Apollo.
You are ancient, yes—
as ancient as every impulse
man struggles to resist.
You would have man remain a child,
punishing him like a child,
frightening him with stories
of what might happen if he's bad.
This is why you take the mother's side.
You want mankind to remain
in a state of infancy,

because then he remains in your power.
If he trusts in his reason,
if he takes justice into his own hands—
then he is lost to you.
You live only if mankind fears you.

Chorus B.
The sun will rise and set
without you, Apollo.
Let the gods banish the Furies,
and soon mankind, with his reason,
will banish the gods.
Soon he will be alone in the universe.
When that happens,
what powers will rise again from his unbelief?
You, Apollo?
Or something deeper,
more primal,
something felt in blood and bone?

(*End of the dance. The court reassembles to hear the verdict. Athena counts the ballots.*)

Athena.
The vote of the jury is tied—
which leaves the deciding vote to me.
I came into this world motherless,
my father's child,
the daughter of Zeus—
formed in the image of his thought.
My judgment is unclouded by a woman's sentiment.
No man can have a claim on me, but in everything else
I hold that a man's claims are strongest.
I side with the father,
and cast my vote to acquit.
Set the prisoner free.

Orestes.
Free.
Finally free from the weight
of death that hung around me like chains.
Goddess Athena:
you have given new life to my house.
For what you have done,
I will honor you all the days of my life.
I will see that justice is done in my own lands,
and between our cities of Argos and Athens
there shall always be peace.

(*Exeunt Orestes and Apollo.*)

Chorus A.
Now you are left with us, goddess—
dishonored, stripped of our ancient rights
by this new kind of justice you proclaim.
You upstart gods
have broken the circle that has been
from the beginning—
the circle of blood.
Our home has always been
in the house of blood,
the house of vengeance—
but you have left us homeless.

Athena. Then make your home here.

Chorus B. Here?

Chorus C.
Where we have been defeated
and dishonored?

Athena.
Be reconciled, and stay with us.

You are ancient powers,
born with Earth and Night,
and you have outlasted the oldest of the gods.
The things you have seen!
The things you know!
But I also have knowledge.
You look into the darkness of men's hearts.
I see them by the light of their best intentions.
Your justice was the justice of the tribe.
Mine is the justice of the city.
You have always honored the dead,
but the world belongs to the living.
For the world to change,
you also must submit to change—
come out of the wilderness
and make your home here.
There is a place for you, underground,
in the foundations of the city.

Chorus A.
Stay here
and become what?
Is this how you mean to mock us—
stripping us of our power,
keeping us here to wither
like shadows in the sun?

Athena.
You have wandered the face of the earth,
feeding on men's iniquity,
with nothing but blood to drink.
I offer you a home,
an end to your wandering.
You will still have great power in the lives of men—
keeping watch over their actions,
binding them to the interests of the state
as before you bound them to the interests of their kin.

Give your power to the city,
and the city will give you honor.

Chorus C.
Only the dead are unchanging—
always as good or evil as death has found them.
For them there is no new beginning.
Agamemnon cannot breathe life
back into the daughter's throat he slit.
Clytemnestra cannot roll up the carpet
that led Agamemnon to his death.
A thousand years, and another thousand—
even eternity cannot make
Aegisthus kind,
Agamemnon gentle,
or Clytemnestra forgiving.

Chorus A. But we are gods.

Chorus B.
If we accept our place in this new world, Athena,
what will our powers be?

Athena.
You will be all-powerful—
watching over the actions of men,
shaping them for service to the state,
shaping them to live their lives for the good of all.
You will become a blessing to the city.

Chorus C.
We are goddesses born of strife—
goddesses of a world still in the bloody pangs
of giving birth to order.
We have seen blood as the end of our work.

Athena.
There is still work for you.

Let the law court become your temple.
Change your cries for blood
to cries for justice.

Chorus A.
We are still convinced of this man's guilt—
this powerful man's son—
but the people have acquitted him.

Chorus B. This is not where justice ends.

Chorus C.
This is our city.
We will not sleep,
we will not be silent,
until there is justice for everyone.

Chorus.

(*Here the Chorus may shed their Fury costumes and appear in "street clothes" for the final procession of the Athenian women. I imagine them in Black Lives Matter T-shirts, Pride T-shirts, etc.*)

We will not sleep.
We will not be silent.

(*The Chorus and dancers form a procession and slowly leave the stage.*)

Athena.
Go, now, women of Athens!
Go, mothers and daughters!
Go back to your homes!

Chorus.
We go with song,
following the footsteps
of each woman who has gone before us.

Athena.
Go, now, women of Athens!
Go, sisters and wives!
Go back to your homes!

Chorus.
We go with song,
carrying the future with us.

Athena.
Go now, women of Athens!
Go ancient children of the Night,
and bless our homes with peace.

End

Notes

1. theh-ous men eye-toe tone dah-pah-lah-gain poe-known
frew-rahs eh-tay-ahs may-kos, hayn koy-mow-men-os
steg-ice Ah-tray-ee-dohn ahng-ka-then kee-nos dee-kayn
kai tous fair-awn-tahs kay-mah kai there-os bro-toys
lahm-prous doon-ahs-tahs em-prep-awn-tahs eye-thair-ee
ah-stair-ahs hoe-tahn fthin-oh-sin ahn-taw-lahs teh tone.

th: as in "thin"
ous: as in "loose"
eh: **e** as in "then"
os: as in "loss"
ah: ă as in "m**o**dest"
ahs: äs as in "**os**cillate"
ai: pronounced like "eye"

Words transliterated as English words (e.g., "tone," "known," "men") should be pronounced like those English words.

2. The Watchman's speech provides the play's *prologos,* or "prologue." The prologue is a common feature of Greek tragedy (sometimes spoken by a god) that sets the stage and introduces the subject of the play. This speech is heavily adapted from Aeschylus to orient a modern audience to the ancient story.

3. Above the main entrance to Agamemnon's citadel of Mycenae is a stone relief of two rampant lions.

4. Aulis, located on the coast of Boeotia in central Greece (see map), is the port from which the Greeks launched their invasion of Troy.

5. Calchas was the principal soothsayer of the Greeks. According to the myth, the goddess Artemis was angry with Agamemnon for killing a deer in her sacred grove, and demanded his daughter Iphigeneia's sacrifice in return before the Greek army could sail to Troy. Achaian: Greek.

6. Much of the backstory here is filled in from Euripides's later tragedy, *Iphigeneia at Aulis*. Iphigeneia was brought to Aulis on the pretext of a marriage to the hero Achilles, but she was instead sacrificed by her father to Artemis.

7. Mt. Ida is a mountain in Turkey, near the site of ancient Troy; Lemnos is a Greek island (modern Limnos) in the northern Aegean; Mt. Athos is a mountain in northeastern Greece. See map. The description of the route of the beacon fires is abridged in this adaptation; Aeschylus names other locations (such as Mt. Kithairon) where the beacon fires were lit.

8. The choral ode sung at the entry of the Chorus is known as the *parodos* (Greek, "entrance"). In this adaptation, individual members of the Chorus enter earlier to join the Watchman, and the rest of the Chorus enters with this ode. In Aeschylus's original, the full Chorus enters after the Watchman's speech.

9. The "messenger speech" is another standard feature of Greek tragedy. The messenger often conveys a message or reports offstage action. But the messenger is more than a convenient device; his speech expressing ambivalence over the Greek victory at Troy reflects one of the underlying themes of the tragedy: that the transition from conflict to order comes with its costs.

10. Nauplion is the port city of Argos (see map).

11. According to myth, Tantalus sacrificed his son Pelops to the gods. He cut up his son's body and served it to the gods at a banquet. The gods realized what they were being served, and caused Pelops to be reassembled

and brought back to life. Pelops gave his name to the Peloponnese, the southern portion of Greece where Argos is located.

12. According to myth, Thyestes in exile raped his daughter Pelopeia, who was the mother of Aegisthus.

13. Helen was the sister of Clytemnestra and the wife of Agamemnon's brother Menelaus. When Helen was abducted by Paris, the son of King Priam of Troy, Agamemnon called together the Greeks to invade Troy and secure the return of Helen.

14. Strophios was the king of Phocis (pronounced *FO-kiss*), a region near the sanctuary of Delphi. He was married to Agamemnon's sister.

15. A Phrygian ally of the Trojans who fell in love with Cassandra and was killed attempting to protect her.

16. In the ancient Greek theater, deaths always took place offstage.

17. Young Electra was omitted in the Hero Now production (2016). In the Carleton production, her character served as a marker of the passage of time; when Electra reappeared (with the words "What a mess"), she wore an identical costume, but an older actress in the role.

18. The second play in Aeschylus's trilogy, *Libation Bearers* (*Choephoroi*) begins with the entrance of Orestes.

19. The scene that follows between Electra and Orestes is known as the "recognition scene," or, in Aristotle's terminology, the *anagnorisis*. In Aeschylus's original, Electra recognizes her brother because he has left a lock of his hair as an offering on Agamemnon's grave, and the hair matches her own; and because he has left footprints which match hers.

20. *Libation Bearers* (*Choephoroi*), took its name from the Chorus of mourners who brought libations to Agamemnon's tomb.

21. The Danaids (daughters of Danaus) killed their husbands on their wedding night and as punishment had to spend eternity attempting to fill

perforated vessels with water. Danaus was one of the mythical founders of Argos.

22. Orestes, in a sense, takes the role of a messenger delivering another messenger speech.

23. In Greek, *Gaia*, or *Gē*.

24. Ouranos (Uranus) was a sky-god and husband of Gaia. His son, Kronos, castrated him, and from the drops of blood the Furies (Erinyes) were formed. Kronos was in turn deposed by his son, Zeus.

25. Delphi was the site of one of the major athletic competitions in the ancient Greek world, the Pythian Games.

26. Pythia, the priestess of Apollo at Delphi and the voice of Apollo's oracle, speaks the prologue in the third play of Aeschylus's trilogy, *Eumenides*. The Furies are the Chorus of the third play.

27. The scene takes place on the Areopagus, a large outcropping of rock to the west of the Acropolis, where the Athenians established the first homicide court.

28. This mention of twelve jurors is an anachronism introduced into the adaptation because the twelve-member jury is a familiar modern institution. In ancient Athens, juries for most trials were very large (500–1000 men). Homicide trials were conducted by the Council of the Areopagus, composed of former *archons* (chief magistrates).

www.ingramcontent.com/pod-product-compliance
Lightning Source LLC
LaVergne TN
LVHW010302260326
834688LV00044B/1415